"The Price of Success: What are you Willing to
Pay For It?"

by Justin & Tia Mason

For more information email:

contact@justintme.com

www.thejustintimebrand.com

DEDICATION

To all current and future entrepreneurs, trailblazers, visionaries and dream chasers: this book is for you. Take a moment to ask yourself these questions: Have you ever felt defeated on your journey to entrepreneurship? Have others laughed at your dreams and doubted your business ideas?

First and foremost, we urge you to keep going. Do not abandon your mission. Are you truly ready to pursue success? Is there anything holding you back? Are you prepared to wait for the right opportunity? Do you have a solid plan in place? Are you willing to make the necessary sacrifices?

As you delve into this book, meditate on these questions. Understand that people will always have opinions on what constitutes success. But remember, it's your journey. Seek your own definition of success and let it guide you.

TABLE OF CONTENTS

~

JUSTIN + TIA – HOW DO YOU DEFINE SUCCESS?

Success has a definition as unique as everyone is. For us, success means defying the odds, standing strong in the face of adversity, embracing humility, and persisting even when others don't understand. True success isn't measured by the money you make, but by the impact you have on people's lives. If your motivation is money alone, you'll fail before you even begin.

Success is about making a difference, leaving a legacy, and touching hearts everywhere you go. Let your drive be the change you want to see in the world, and you'll find that success will follow.

INTRODUCTION

Grace and peace to every reader who opens this book. I hope the stories within these pages will inspire and motivate you on your entrepreneurial journey. My name is Justin, and I am honored to serve as the CEO of Just-In Time, a company born from faith and perseverance.

In 2016, Just-In Time began as a humble cleaning service. Today, it has grown into a multifaceted enterprise, including Just In-Time Cleaning Services, Just In-Time Auto Detailing, Just In-Time Investments, and Just In-Time Consulting. This growth did not come easy. My wife and I face countless rejections, adversity, and obstacles.

We knew deep in our hearts what God had promised us. In 2017, when deciding capital was necessary for growth and sustainability, we confidently approached the bank for a loan to expand our business. My wife passionately shared our vision, detailing our plans with unwavering belief. The banker, however, dismissed us coldly, stating, "You will only be a mom-and-pop shop."

That moment could have shattered our dreams. Instead, it ignited a fire within us. We knew our worth wasn't defined by a banker's opinion but by our Creator's vision for us. That dismissal pushed us out of our comfort zone and into God's will. We had no business plan, no formal background in entrepreneurship, but we had faith and determination.

This book is a testament to the struggles and triumphs of our journey. It's a reminder that success comes at a price, often requiring you to rise above doubt and defy the odds. Join us as we explore the highs and lows, the rejections and victories, and discover the true essence of what it takes to succeed. Do you have what it takes to #keepgoing?

The Price of Success: What are you Willing to Pay?

CHAPTER 1:
What is Success?

This is the million-dollar question, isn't it? Webster defines success as "a person or thing that achieves desired aims or attains prosperity." But what does this definition mean to you? Often, we look at others and try to figure out how to duplicate their achievements. But in many instances, what they have done cannot be duplicated because, simply put, you are not them. Sounds harsh, doesn't it?

But it's reality. God has made each of us different in our own way. Think about it—no two human beings have the same set of fingerprints. So why do we try so hard to make someone else's dreams our reality?

There is nothing wrong with learning what made others successful, but have you ever thought about putting the same effort into researching your own success instead of theirs? What is it that you want to do?

Consider Michelle Obama's words in the quote below. She sat beside President Obama in some of the most coveted seats in life. They will never have to worry about finances again. Read her quote and think about its powerful simplicity. In life, many of us are taught that money is the solution to all our problems. And whilst it is true that money can solve many issues, the reality is, money is dangerous when you lack the discipline to manage it.

I think back to when my wife and I started Just-In Time. We had big dreams and goals that we were determined to achieve. There was so much excitement we shared; little did we know, with our excitement came adversity. We were told that our business would just be a mom-and-pop shop. We knew what God had shown us, and we had to persevere and trust His plan for our business; we had an unwavering "knowing" it was Just-In Time. We were "Just-In Time" for God's plan for our lives, "Just-In Time" to ignore the opinions of others. It was time for us to operate out of obedience and not fear, and now we are here to help you.

What are you "Just-In Time" for? In an industry where others have succeeded and failed, what are you going to do differently? What will motivate you to achieve your goals? How will you accomplish what no one else thinks is possible? What is your ultimate "why"? Your success will be for more than just you. I am talking to husbands and wives pursuing entrepreneurship together, friends, people engaged to be married, single folks—everyone.

You must realize that sometimes God uses you as an example for others. This often means making sacrifices that others will not. At the end of Michelle Obama's statement, she speaks about the difference you make in other people's lives. Every great Founder/CEO knows this secret: no matter how great the company becomes; it did not happen without help. Your dream will only go as far as your team! It took a great deal of sacrifice to create opportunities for all the employees. Understand this: an entrepreneur cannot be selfish. When you achieve your goals, do not frown upon the people and sacrifices that got you there.

One thing that amazes me about Ford Motor Company is how they issue profit-sharing checks to all their employees every year. This is the CEO's acknowledgment that without their workers, there can be no success. Do not let your pursuit of success rob you of your effort. Why? Because if your effort quits on you, what will replace it?

We need to realize that we are more capable than we give ourselves credit for. One of the most underrated things is our imagination. You must visualize it first. Our company started with a vision.

The manifestation of my vision did not come until my wife Tia helped me prioritize what to do first. God played a crucial role, but He also showed me I needed help. Even if you are not married or in a relationship, do not forget to work towards your vision.

Faith without works is dead. Do not let your vision die due to lack of action. Faith alone will not move God!

Success does not have a taste that everyone likes; it is an acquired taste. It is not always about the taste of the food but about suppressing the appetite. The journey to success may not always taste good, but if allowed, it can achieve its goal: to suppress the urge to fall into the "get rich quick gimmicks". Go back and find the passion that drove you. Do not scrap your ideas; dust them off and critique them.

Reflecting on my adolescent days, Proverbs 23:7 states, "For as he thinketh in his heart, so is he." Ask yourself what your thoughts are right now. Whatever you are meditating on is what you will produce. Often, this is the time when fear, doubt, and worry arise. I remember being so afraid to start this company. My biggest fear was consistency. If things worked out immediately, I felt confident. But when they did not, I felt abandoned, alone, and afraid.

I am not ashamed to let you know my faults because I have learned how to GROW from them. I was always concerned about what others thought I should or could have done. I did not fully trust and rely on God. Yes, I serve Him and live for Him, but I still had to go through my own valley to appreciate the heights of the mountaintop. People may see where I am today, but every journey has a story. If I had given up in the early days, there would only be a story of failure.

Do not give up, no matter how hard it gets. Your story is going to help in ways you did not think was possible. You are more than capable of achieving your goals. Believe in yourself because if you don't, who will? Find your motivation. Understand that success starts in the mind. What seeds have you allowed to be planted? You must,

"see it" before you see it. Look past the temporary and focus on the permanent.

Instead of just meditating on dreams, meditate on your goals as well. Money may motivate you, but what is driving you? Your seed (vision) can never be planted if it stays in the package. Your next step is critical not only for yourself but for others as well. Every great athlete will tell you who inspired them. My greatest inspiration has been God.

Everything around you has a purpose; draw inspiration from both negativity and positivity. Romans 8:28 states, "And we know that all things work together for good to them that love God, to them who are the called according to His purpose."

You are more than capable of overcoming your struggles and setbacks. Yes, you, the one who feels counted out, laughed at, talked about, maybe on your second or third try, or maybe more. Look in the mirror and tell yourself it had to happen like that so that God could get the glory out of it. Walk into this next season of your life with purpose and focus.

Passion, Desire, and Love will hold you up during the struggles, trials and tribulations, embrace every part of the journey. It will be well worth it when it becomes reality. The fact that you are considering following your dreams is a victory. You have not let your dreams die! Trailblazers are those rare visionaries who don't just navigate uncharted territories, they redefine them. As you read this book, if you are currently in a place of success, congratulations – don't stop climbing! If you're in a place of obtaining success, remember these days as they will be monumental to not only you, but the others coming behind you.

Remember, you had to start somewhere - which caused you to tread territories that were once unfamiliar. Failure, Frustration, Fatigue, or sickness does NOT give you permission to quit! My wife and I have dealt with them all, but we're mandated to hold on to the mantra of #keepgoing; if we must, so do you!

1. What does success mean to you?

_____

_____

_____

_____

_____

_____

_____

_____

_____

_____

_____

_____

_____

_____

_____

_____

_____

_____

_____

_____

_____

_____

_____

_____

_____

_____

_____

_____

_____

2. What do you think you are, "Just-In-Time" for? What is God trying to do in your life?

_____

_____

_____

_____

_____

_____

_____

_____

_____

_____

_____

_____

_____

_____

_____

_____

_____

_____

_____

_____

_____

_____

_____

_____

_____

_____

_____

_____

CHAPTER 2: Conversations with the Past

Have you ever wondered what life would be like if the older you could go back and talk to the younger you? Imagine the possibilities. How successful would we be if we could have stopped ourselves from making those foolish decisions? I used to think this way until I realized something profound— I am a byproduct of my experiences, both good and bad. If you go back and change what you've been through, you change who you are. Our experiences shape our identities.

Here's an analogy I've come to understand: a mirror never lies. It shows you everything that's right and wrong without apology. Some of us need to invest in a metaphorical mirror. What does that mean? It means you must look within yourself and examine your faults. And when you find them, work on them! I'm not saying it will change immediately, but nothing will change if you don't start working on the things that need improvement. Success requires self-awareness and the willingness to confront uncomfortable truths about us.

When you look at success, you must realize this: failure lives right next door. Many people run from failure because of its side effects. But have you ever considered this crazy thought? Failure is a key ingredient in success. There isn't a single person walking this earth who is successful and hasn't experienced failure.

We are taught to fear failure, but why? The sad reality is that we fear failure because of how it looks. Life is about simple choices that we sometimes make hard. Yet, we often remain comfortable with just dreaming instead of doing. Don't let doubt take the seat of confidence in your life!

You've worked so hard to get to this place, right? Then why give up so easily just because it doesn't work immediately? These questions don't require answers from only yourself. If at first you fail, try again, and again until you find what makes it work for you! Giving up is not an option. I remember honestly wanting to quit my entrepreneurial journey. I was seriously considering job offers from other employers.

One job offered a $1,500 signing bonus! To some people, that may seem insignificant, but to me, as a struggling father, husband, and man, it was the equivalent of winning the lottery. I was excited! I went into the house and began to tell my wife the great news. She looked at me with the straightest face and said, "No."

That moment was a turning point. I was fighting with my faith, believing my plan was better than the one God had for me. But that day marked the beginning of my true journey of faith. I realized that what I thought was an easy way out was a test of my commitment and belief in the vision I had. My wife's refusal to let me settle was a reminder that faith is not truly faith until it has been tested beyond its limits.

You see, what I'm trying to convey is that your faith must be tested to be genuine. It's easy to believe when everything is going well, but real faith is forged in the fires of adversity. Embrace your journey, with all its trials and failures, because they are the very experiences that will shape you into the person you are meant to be.

I want to share something with you all; if anyone knows Tia and I, they know our stance on transparency. It's a critical component in the evolution of those coming behind you! The years 2016 and 2017 were some of the hardest of our lives. We had no real business plan, no solid business background, and our partner at the time from Just-In Time Cleaning had just overcome a massive health scare that landed him in the hospital.

We were learning the cleaning industry on the fly, working for pennies, and constantly being told our worth instead of knowing it ourselves. Heartaches came from trusted people, we questioned and doubted ourselves, and there were times when we worked without being paid. We didn't even have the money to buy adequate cleaning supplies—Dollar Tree was our best friend. I felt deeply ashamed of my inability to adequately care for my pregnant wife, and we felt painfully underprepared for the business God had instructed us to start.

Through tears and pain, we knew there was only one option: to persevere. We had to stand on God's promises in the face of adversity. We paved the way for the next entrepreneur, for those who think it's impossible, for those who are fearful, for those who are discouraged, and for those on the brink of throwing in the towel. We stood and still stand for those individuals.

Writing this book is exciting because it allows us to share the critical pieces of our lives that have defined who we are today. But during this process, we quickly realized how much it hurts to remember the past. The struggles we faced, the pain we endured, and the doubts that plagued us are all still fresh in our minds. Yet, these experiences are as relevant and necessary in 2025 as they were in 2016.

We still remember the days when we were laughed at and told we would never succeed. We remember the sleepless nights, the days we couldn't afford proper meals, and the times we questioned whether it was all worth it. We had moments of despair, where giving up seemed like the easier option. But in those moments, we clung to the belief that we were on this journey for a reason, that our struggles were not in vain, and that we had a higher purpose to fulfill.

We now understand that our journey was not just about us. It was about paving the way for others, showing them that it is possible to overcome seemingly insurmountable odds. It was about being a beacon of hope for those who are struggling, showing them that perseverance, faith, and hard work can lead to success. Our story is a testament to the power of resilience and the importance of never giving up, no matter how tough the road gets.

As we continue this journey, our advice for the next entrepreneur is simple: cling to humility, write a vision board, and never give up. You must see it before you actually see it. Visualize your goals, and let that vision drive you forward. Even when it seems crazy to keep going, even when the odds are stacked against you, keep pushing forward.

We share our story not to boast, but to inspire. We want you to know that you are not alone in your struggles. Every great success story has moments of doubt, fear, and pain. But it is through these moments that we find our true strength. Our journey is far from over, and we continue to face challenges. But we move forward with the knowledge that we have overcome so much already, and we can overcome whatever comes next.

We hope our story serves as a reminder that success is not a straight path, but a winding road filled with highs and lows, and that you, too, have the power to walk this road and achieve your dreams. #keepgoing

1. What vision do you have for your life?

_____

_____

_____

_____

_____

_____

_____

_____

_____

_____

_____

_____

_____

_____

_____

_____

_____

_____

_____

_____

_____

_____

_____

_____

_____

_____

_____

_____

_____

_____

_____

_____

2.   What steps will you take to get there?

Step 1

_____
_____
_____
_____
_____
_____
_____
_____

Step 2

_____
_____
_____
_____
_____
_____
_____
_____

Step 3

_____
_____
_____
_____
_____
_____
_____

CHAPTER 3: The Power of Motivation, Courage, Determination & Knowledge

Let's talk **Motivation**, what is it? The reason or reasons one has for acting or behaving in a way.

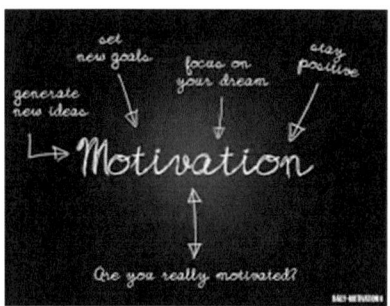

One of the most powerful and underrated stories in the Bible is about the man we call "Doubting Thomas." In this passage, we see a man struggling to believe what his fellow disciples are saying.

Imagine for a moment how they met him at the door with such excitement, ready to share their incredible experience and expecting Thomas to join in their joy. But instead of matching their enthusiasm, he responded with skepticism, essentially saying, "Man, y'all are trippin'. Unless I see it for myself, I cannot join in on all this excitement!"

Can I ask you this question? How would you have responded if you were in Thomas's shoes? How was he so close to his fellow disciples yet so distant at the same time, supposedly cut from the same cloth but unable to share in their faith? The disciples were not lying about seeing Jesus, but neither was Thomas wrong in needing his own proof.

Here is my issue with people who act like they've never experienced doubt: we've all been there! We have all doubted what we could not see while believing what we've heard and felt. Christ told them all that after three days, He would rise again. But He never specified how He would reveal Himself. When the disciples saw Him, it must have felt like déjà vu, a reminder of the conversations they had. Let me speak from two perspectives:

To those with a message for, "Thomas the Doubter": don't be upset when others don't see things the way you do. It wasn't their time to experience what you did. He said it, you believe it, and that settles it. To my so-called doubters: it is okay to need proof of what you believe. You do not need an explanation when you can experience it for yourself.

When you have self-motivation, nothing else matters. It reminds me of one of my favorite Lauryn Hill songs, "Nothing Even Matters." Before I get carried away, let's get back to the story. Some of you may not know about her, but the point is to open your mind to both doubt and belief; then make a comparison like Thomas did. He had the choice to go along with the narrative or to change it.

Many people might wonder why he could not just get excited and join in, instead of marching to the beat of his own drum. Even though a band has many instruments, each one is designed to make its own sound. I don't expect the drummer to sound like the piano or saxophone, correct? But what we need to hear is the harmony between the instruments. Even though Jesus called out Thomas's doubt, I must thank Thomas for his transparency.

Starting and running these companies is one thing but maintaining them is a whole different beast! There have been many days and nights of wrestling with doubt and belief at the same time.

To all the spiritually strong people who've never dealt with this struggle, let me remind you of the man in the Book of Mark who said these exact words to Jesus concerning his son's situation: "Lord, I do believe; help my unbelief." It is okay to admit that even though we believe we can accomplish our goals, there's something that also makes us doubt.

Whether it's a lack of money, failed attempts from the past, not living up to others' expectations, not being in the place you thought you'd be in by now, or something else – we all have our reasons. But do not harp on to all the negative thoughts. Even if I have 99% doubt, I hold on to that 1% chance of belief. That's what keeps us going. When I think about giving up, I also think about what if I don't give up. What if that 1% belief is all I need to tip the scales in my favor? What if perseverance through doubt leads to success?

Thomas's story teaches us that doubt is not the enemy; it's part of the journey. His skepticism wasn't a weakness, but a step towards a stronger, more resilient faith. Likewise, our doubts and fears are not signs of failure, but opportunities to deepen our resolve and fortify our belief in our goals. When you stand on the edge of doubt, remember that the other side of that chasm is belief and possibility. So, embrace your doubts. They make your journey real and your successes even sweeter. Each step, whether driven by faith or hesitation, brings you closer to your dreams. Remember, it is not the absence of doubt that defines success but the determination to move forward despite it. As we continue this path, let us hold on to that 1% belief and let it drive us to greatness.

Next, let's address Courage, what is it? The ability to do something that frightens one.

The Six Types of Courage

Physical Courage: To keep going with resiliency, balance & awareness.
Social Courage: To be yourself unapologetically.
Moral Courage: Doing the right thing even when it's uncomfortable or unpopular
Emotional Courage: Feeling all your emotions (positive & negative) without guilt or attachment.
Intellectual Courage: to learn, unlearn and relearn with an open & flexible mind.
Spiritual Courage: Living with purpose & meaning through a heart centered approach towards all life and oneself.

Starting the business took immense courage and shook us to our core. We were comfortable with the security of our daily jobs, the guaranteed paychecks every two weeks, and my weekly income. The decision to pursue entrepreneurship meant abandoning all that comfort for an uncertain future.

It was an all-or-nothing leap, a choice to leave everything behind and follow our passion. The fear of the unknown was paralyzing, but we knew we had to take the plunge.

Leaving behind the stability we had always known for the uncharted waters of business ownership required a level of bravery we hadn't realized we possessed. It meant stepping into the unknown, risking everything for a dream. If that isn't the essence of courage, then I don't know what is. Our journey began with this bold move, fueled by determination and a relentless pursuit of our passion. I once heard it put like this:

"If your dreams don't scare you, they're too small"!

Now we're moving on to **Determination,** what is it? Firmness of purpose; resoluteness."

DETERMINATION
is doing what
needs to be done
even when you don't
feel like doing it.

Impossible is just something no one has done yet. Think of Noah, who looked utterly crazy building an ark for a flood that seemed impossible in his current situation. He built it anyway, so when the time came, he was prepared. You must decide whether fear or faith will determine your vision. Will you let fear cloud your sight, or will you let faith illuminate the possibilities?

When you face a storm, remember these three truths: storms are temporary, storms are teachers, and storms are transportation devices to your destiny. Some of the greatest ship captains earned their honor not by navigating calm seas but by steering through relentless storms. These challenges honed their skills and proved their mettle. Are you ready to build for your future? Embrace the storm, for it is shaping you into the architect of a future that others will look up to for inspiration. You might just be laying the foundation for those who will follow in your footsteps.

Let's finish here with **Knowledge**, what is it? Facts, information, and skills acquired by a person through experience or education, the theoretical or practical understanding of a subject. Understanding and embracing fearlessness is essential to overcoming the mindset that you cannot achieve the unthinkable.

Turn your setbacks into opportunities for comebacks. Take control of your life and get back on the road to success. I remember a day vividly when I had just gotten a newer vehicle. While driving on the freeway, I experienced a tire blowout. In that moment, I was a whirlwind of emotions: mad, frustrated, embarrassed, and nervous all at once.

What eased my mind a bit was knowing I had a spare tire in my trunk. It wasn't ideal, but it was enough to get me moving again. This spare tire represents your backup plan or idea. If you have that spare idea, you can get back on the road. However, it's crucial to understand that a spare is only temporary. It's a means to keep going, but not a permanent solution.

While using your spare tire, remember that you must replace it with the main tire eventually. This illustration serves to remind you that excuses are useless when you have the resources to continue. There have been countless times when I needed a divine pep talk to keep me going. I have been on the brink of quitting and returning to a 9-5 job. There is no condemnation for those who work a traditional schedule; my focus here is to encourage you to push through those moments of doubt. It's perfectly okay to have a moment of weakness, to feel overwhelmed and uncertain. What matters is how you respond to that moment.

During those low points, I've learned that our greatest victories often come after our hardest battles. The key is to keep moving forward, even if it means relying on a temporary solution until you can find a more permanent fix. Life will throw unexpected obstacles in your path, but how you handle them will define your journey. Your setbacks do not define you; your comebacks do.

Every challenge you face is an opportunity to build resilience, gain wisdom, and prove to yourself that you are capable of more than you ever imagined. So, take a deep breath, trust in your spare tire when needed, but always strive to replace it with something stronger.

Your road to success may be bumpy, but each obstacle is a step towards your ultimate destination. Remember, the journey is just as important as the destination, and every detour can lead to new insights and growth. Keep driving forward with courage and determination. #keepgoing

"Success is a journey,
not a destination...."

What is something you need courage to do?

_____

_____

_____

_____

_____

_____

_____

_____

_____

_____

_____

_____

_____

_____

_____

_____

_____

_____

_____

_____

_____

_____

_____

_____

_____

_____

_____

_____

_____

_____

_____

_____

_____

CHAPTER 4: You Must Put a Down Payment on Your Future

Investing in your future is like placing a down payment on a life-altering purchase. That initial investment, your effort, time, and faith—is the foundation upon which everything else is built. How much are you willing to invest in your dreams? Success requires a price, and that price is not paid in comfort or convenience but in persistence, resilience, and determination.

Think of it this way: who values their paycheck more, the one who earns it through hard work or the one to whom it is simply given? The former understands the cost, the sacrifice, and the perseverance it took to attain it. The latter may lack that same appreciation because they didn't have to fight for it.

This principle extends to every pursuit in life. Too often, we declare that we're willing to do whatever it takes to succeed, yet as soon as adversity strikes, we retreat to what feels safe. The reality is many people are not truly prepared for the trials success demands.

When your effort doesn't immediately yield results, it's tempting to give up. You might feel empty, as though all the work was for nothing. But here's the truth: mental surrender is the precursor to physical defeat. Dreams don't die in the face of challenges—they die when we stop believing in their possibility. Every mother who has endured the pain of childbirth knows this.

I vividly recall standing in the delivery room with my wife, watching her labor through agony and exhaustion. Yet despite the pain, she didn't stop. She pushed through, and her perseverance gave us the beautiful gift of life, our son.

That experience taught me a lesson that resonates far beyond parenthood. Success is birthed in the same way—through pain, struggle, and relentless effort. You may not see the results immediately, but the process is shaping you, refining you, and preparing you for what's to come. Success has its own timetable, and you must be ready to deliver when the moment arrives. If you stay ready, you will not have to get ready.

Rooted in Patience

Success begins as a seed. A small, seemingly insignificant act of faith planted in fertile ground. But here's the thing about seeds: they don't sprout overnight. Any farmer or gardener knows this. A seed must first develop roots, anchoring itself deeply into the soil before it can break through the surface. In the same way, your efforts must take root in patience, persistence, and preparation.

Patience is not optional; it is a prerequisite for growth. You cannot rush the process of success, nor can you cheat it. The only person you cheat is yourself. Just like in school, where shortcuts may get you through one test but leave you unprepared for the next, life will expose any foundation that isn't built on integrity and effort. The question isn't whether you'll face challenges, it's whether you'll be ready for them when they come.

The Unseen Work

Many people fail before they even begin because they are fixated on the problem rather than the possibilities. They see the challenge and assume there's no solution, disqualifying themselves before they've even tried. But here's the secret: effort is your greatest asset. It may not sound glamorous, but it is the engine that transforms dreams into reality. Effort is the down payment on your future.

Think about it—effort is the one thing entirely within your control. It's not dependent on circumstances, resources, or the opinions of others. When you show up and give your all, you're not just working toward your goals; you're proving to yourself that you are capable of far more than you imagined.

Faith in the Process

Faith is taking the first step before God reveals the second. It's trusting that the seed you've planted will grow, even when you can't yet see any evidence. Faith requires you to push through the dirt, the delays, and the disappointments. It demands that you act as though the promise is already fulfilled, even when it feels impossibly distant.

But faith without work is dead. You can believe in your dreams all you want, but if you don't pair that belief with action, it will remain just that—a dream. Action is what turns hope into a plan and faith into fulfillment.

The Price of Success

The journey to success will test you. It will challenge your patience, your discipline, and your resolve. But remember, every sacrifice, every setback, and every sleepless night is part of the price. The question is not whether the price is worth paying, it's whether you're willing to pay it.

Success doesn't come to those who wait passively; it comes to those who prepare actively. It's not about luck or timing, it's about showing up every day with the determination to make your dream a reality. So, plant your seeds. Nurture them with effort, water them with faith, and trust that in due time, they will grow into something extraordinary. Your future is waiting. What down payment will you make today?

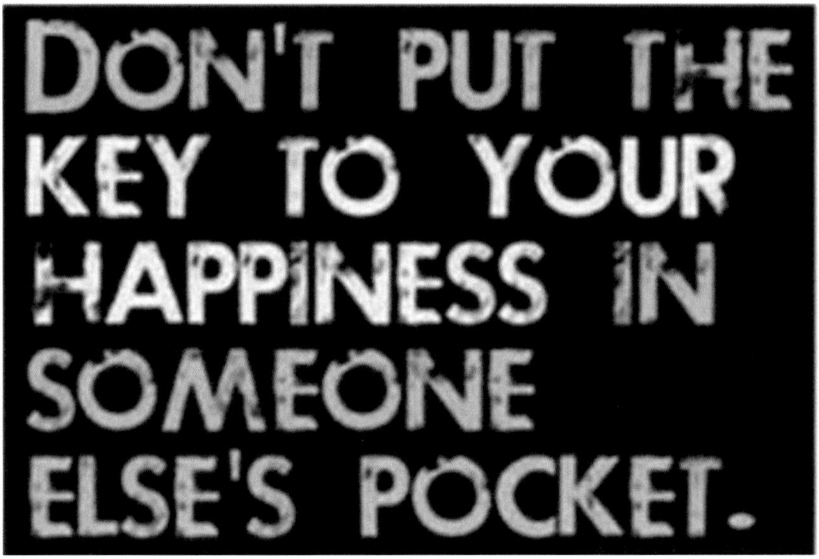
DON'T PUT THE
KEY TO YOUR
HAPPINESS IN
SOMEONE
ELSE'S POCKET.

What Challenges are keeping you from reaching your goals?

_____

_____

_____

_____

_____

_____

_____

_____

_____

_____

_____

_____

_____

_____

_____

_____

_____

_____

_____

_____

_____

_____

_____

_____

_____

_____

_____

_____

_____

_____

_____

_____

_____

CHAPTER 5: The Dynamic Duo: Entrepreneurs and Intrapreneurs

One of the greatest questions you can ask yourself is: which one were you meant to be, an entrepreneur or an intrapreneur? Want to know a secret? Whichever answer you choose is the right one. Understand this: an entrepreneur needs an intrapreneur just as much as an intrapreneur needs an entrepreneur. What is an entrepreneur? At its core, an entrepreneur is a visionary. A trailblazer who steps into the unknown, armed with little more than faith, determination, and an unshakable belief in the possibilities ahead. Entrepreneurs birth ideas that disrupt industries, transform lives, and create opportunities where none existed. They are risk-takers, dreamers, and builders, willing to venture into uncharted territories to make their vision a reality. But here's the truth that many don't tell you: even the most dynamic entrepreneurs cannot do it alone.

This is where the intrapreneur steps in. An intrapreneur is the heartbeat within the body of a vision. They work within the framework of the entrepreneur's dream, acting as the hands and feet that bring the vision to life. While the entrepreneur often operates at 30,000 feet—dreaming, strategizing, and planning—the intrapreneur is on the ground, executing, innovating, and ensuring the foundation is solid. They thrive within the walls of a structure, refining processes, managing teams, and finding ways to add value. An intrapreneur doesn't just work for the vision—they adopt it as their own.

Entrepreneurs and intrapreneurs are not competitors; they are complements. They need each other in ways that are both profound and practical. The entrepreneur is the spark that ignites the flame, but the intrapreneur is the one who keeps it burning. Without an entrepreneur's vision, an intrapreneur has no direction. Without an intrapreneur's dedication, an entrepreneur's dream may remain a lofty idea, never grounded in reality. Together, they create a synergy that moves mountains and turns dreams into tangible success.

Consider the example of Moses and Aaron from the Bible. Moses was the visionary, chosen by God to lead the Israelites out of Egypt. But he couldn't do it alone. Aaron became his mouthpiece, his support, and his partner in carrying out the mission. The two were inseparable in purpose. Similarly, every entrepreneur needs an intrapreneur—a partner who can help carry the load, speak the vision into existence, and manage the challenges that inevitably arise.

This relationship is not one-sided. Just as an entrepreneur needs an intrapreneur, the intrapreneur benefits immensely from the entrepreneur's ability to see what others cannot. Entrepreneurs create environments that allow intrapreneurs to innovate and thrive. They provide the vision, the structure, and the challenges that intrapreneurs need to grow. Intrapreneurs, in turn, build on that foundation, becoming indispensable to the success of the business.

So, if you are an entrepreneur, ask yourself: Who is my intrapreneur? Who can I trust to help carry the vision forward, someone who is as invested in the dream as I am? And if you're an intrapreneur, consider this: How can I serve the vision I've been entrusted with, and how can I contribute to its success in a way that makes me indispensable?

The truth is, God designed us to need each other. Entrepreneurs and intrapreneurs are like the two sides of a coin, different but inseparable. Together, they can accomplish what neither could achieve alone. Whether you're a visionary entrepreneur or the committed intrapreneur, the world needs what you bring to the table.

This concept forces us to rethink how we approach relationships, especially in business and leadership. It challenges us to move past the myth of the self-made individual. No matter how brilliant, passionate, or capable you are, there will always be gaps you cannot fill alone. That's not a weakness; it's God's design. He created us to work in collaboration, to reflect His divine order through our partnerships. Entrepreneurs and intrapreneurs embody this design—they are living testimonies to the power of unity.

Think about this on a personal level. Are you trying to do it all on your own? Are you carrying the weight of the vision without inviting others to help build it? It's easy to feel like asking for help is a sign of weakness or that no one else can understand your passion for the dream. But God didn't call you to carry the entire load. He placed people in your life—potential intrapreneurs—who are equipped to help you. The question is, do you trust them enough to let them?

In the next set of passages, we will challenge you to see leadership and intrapreneurship not just as roles but as opportunities to grow, serve, and achieve your God-given purpose. As we move forward, remember this: ***Greatness is not found in doing it all by yourself—it is found in doing it together.***

The Heart of Leadership and the Spirit of Intrapreneurship:

What does it truly mean to lead? And what does it mean to follow with intention, influence, and integrity? These questions lie at the heart of understanding leadership and intrapreneurship. Both roles, though distinct, share a common thread: the ability to inspire, serve, and cultivate growth in others while advancing a vision far bigger than oneself.

Leadership is often misunderstood as dominance, control, or the ability to command a crowd. But true leadership, as exemplified by figures like Jesus, is rooted in servanthood. Jesus led not by lording His power over others but by humbling Himself, washing feet, feeding the hungry, and teaching with wisdom and compassion.

He didn't seek followers; His heart to serve attracted them. In the same way, the most effective leaders in business, ministry, and life don't lead from ego—they lead from empathy. Leadership is not about the position you hold but the posture of your heart.

On the other hand, intrapreneurship is the unsung hero of any successful endeavor.

Intrapreneurs are silent architects who take the leader's vision and build upon it with ingenuity, dedication, and excellence. Their work often happens behind the scenes, but their impact is profound. Intrapreneurs possess a unique quality: they can see the bigger picture while mastering the details. They don't just execute orders; they innovate, challenge the status quo, and breathe life into the vision. But here's the truth that often goes unspoken: Leadership and intrapreneurship are not titles you're given—they're traits you develop. Whether you're the one casting the vision or the one building it, the qualities that define these roles must be cultivated intentionally.

Leadership: From Visionary to Vessel

To lead effectively, you must first lead yourself. True leadership begins with self-awareness. Ask yourself: *What drives me? What are my strengths and weaknesses? Am I willing to confront the areas of my life that need growth?* A leader who is unwilling to grow will stunt the growth of everyone they lead.

Next, leadership requires vision. But vision without action is a fantasy. A true leader doesn't just dream—they plan, execute, and adapt. They are not afraid to take risks, make mistakes, and learn from failure. They understand that leadership is a journey of continual refinement, not a destination.

Most importantly, a leader must be a listener. Listening is the bridge between vision and action, between the leader and the team. It is through listening that a leader gains the trust, respect, and insights needed to move the vision forward.

Intrapreneurship: The Power of Ownership

If leadership is the head of an organization, intrapreneurship is its heartbeat. Intrapreneurs thrive when they take ownership of their role, treating it as if the vision were their own. This mindset transforms a mere task into a mission and elevates an employee to a vital contributor.

To cultivate the spirit of intrapreneurship, you must embrace responsibility. Stop waiting for someone to hand you the blueprint and start creating solutions. Intrapreneurs are proactive, not reactive. They don't just see problems; they see opportunities for innovation.

Another essential quality of intrapreneurship is humility. It takes humility to work in the shadow of someone else's vision. But in that humility lies strength. Intrapreneurs understand that their work is significant, even if it doesn't always come with recognition.

The Synergy Between the Two

Leadership and intrapreneurship are not opposing forces—they are complementary. When a leader casts a vision with clarity and conviction, they create a space where intrapreneurs can thrive. When intrapreneurs bring their full creativity and commitment to the table, they strengthen the leader's vision and make it a reality. This synergy reminds us that no one can succeed in isolation. Even Moses needed Aaron to hold up his arms during the battle. Even Paul relied on Timothy to carry out his mission. Every leader needs an intrapreneur, and every intrapreneur needs a leader.

Applying These Qualities to Your Life

As you reflect on the qualities of leadership and intrapreneurship, consider where you stand. Are you a visionary who needs to sharpen your ability to communicate and inspire? Or are you the builder who needs to step up with greater confidence and ownership?

Write down the traits you admire most in leaders and intrapreneurs you respect. Then, ask yourself: *How can I embody these qualities in my own journey?* Begin with small, intentional steps. Lead by serving others. Innovate in your current role. Take ownership of your responsibilities as if they were your own vision.

"It is hard to follow someone who is not in front of you."

~Brenda Mason Brown

Are you an entrepreneur or an intrapreneur?

_____
_____
_____
_____
_____
_____
_____
_____
_____
_____
_____
_____
_____
_____
_____
_____
_____
_____
_____
_____
_____
_____
_____
_____
_____
_____
_____
_____
_____
_____
_____
_____
_____
_____
_____
_____
_____
_____
_____
_____

CHAPTER 6: Building While You're Waiting

Ecclesiastes 3:1 *"To everything there is a season, and a time to every purpose under the heaven."*

I t's a simple truth, yet one that's incredibly hard to live by. Why? Because it touches on something we all struggle with—patience. This verse tells us there is a season for everything, and just like a farmer knows when to plant, there's a time for you to sow seeds in your life and wait for them to take root.

Think about a farmer, patiently tilling the soil, knowing that his seeds won't sprout right away. The seed first must take root before anything begins to grow. No matter how much water or sunlight it receives, the timing must be right for it to flourish. Sometimes, we get impatient. We want results fast. We think if the results don't come quickly enough, it's time to abandon the effort. But here's where patience becomes crucial, anything worth having is worth waiting for.

The farmer understands this. When the season is right, he will see the fruits of his labor. Imagine the satisfaction of seeing a fully grown crop, knowing it's the result of careful planning, hard work, and patience. That feeling of fulfillment comes only after enduring the waiting period.

Now, I'm not saying you must become a farmer, but apply the same effort to your dreams. You don't have to wait until it physically manifests to start believing in it. You must see it in your mind first. That mental vision is what will carry you through the waiting season.

But don't get me wrong—just because you see it mentally doesn't mean it'll happen overnight. Patience is a key ingredient in turning dreams into reality. Every beautiful creation you see—whether it's art, architecture, or a successful business—took time to build. The process for some may be slower than for others, but if you keep working, keep believing, it will happen for you.

Think of it this way: without an architect laying out the plans, no building can be constructed. God is the master architect of our lives. He has already drawn up the blueprint, but it's up to us to follow the plan, brick by brick. Even when it seems like nothing is happening, or the progress is too slow, trust that the foundation is being laid beneath the surface.

You have probably heard the saying, *"You miss 100% of the shots you don't take."* That's true in life, too. Every missed shot is an opportunity to learn, to adjust, to aim better next time. Don't give up after a few misses. Keep pushing, keep taking those shots. When opportunity knocks, be ready to answer. Make sure you are prepared, because the more prepared you are, the more opportunities will come knocking.

Here is another thing to consider, visionaries see what others can't. What can you see about yourself that others don't? Stop letting yourself down by doubting what you're capable of. Surround yourself with people who share your vision and who are on the same path as you. If you want to be a carpenter, don't spend your time with people studying to become electricians. While their journey might be important, it's not aligned with yours. Stay focused on your path and surround yourself with those who are walking alongside you. *"Can two walk together, unless they are agreed?" Amos 3:3*

Opportunities can often look like empty, abandoned buildings—run down, forgotten, and in need of a lot of work. But those buildings are waiting for someone with vision to come along and turn them into something beautiful. Every day that passes is a missed opportunity to start building. It's time to invest in yourself. Who knows? You might be the next person to create something incredible, the next big idea that changes everything.

Remember, you are just one innovative thought away from making a difference in the world. You could also be the person holding the key to unlock someone else's potential. The quickest way to kill a big dream is to introduce it to a small mind. Don't let that happen to you. Keep your dreams alive by feeding them with vision, effort, and persistence.

You can't expect different results if you keep doing the same things. Change your habits. Change your environment. Invest in yourself. Find a mentor, someone who's walked the path before you, and learn from them. Do what you need to do now, so you can live the life you want later. The waiting period is not wasted time—it's building time. And when your season arrives, all the work you've put in will reveal something beautiful. So, ask yourself: Are you ready to build while you wait? Because the time is now!

1. **Visionaries see what others can't. What can you see about yourself that others don't?**

_____
_____
_____
_____
_____
_____
_____
_____
_____
_____
_____
_____
_____
_____
_____
_____
_____
_____
_____
_____
_____
_____
_____
_____
_____
_____
_____
_____
_____
_____
_____
_____
_____
_____

CHAPTER 7:
Prophetic Preparation

What does ,"prophetic preparation" look like to you? For us, it meant stepping into the unknown with unwavering faith, preparing in the very areas where God was calling us to grow, even when it didn't make sense. It meant taking action in the midst of the storm. In April of 2024, God spoke a word over us: "There's a demand for your development." At that time, we had no idea what He truly meant, but little did we know we were about to embark on one of the most challenging seasons of our lives.

Between 2023 and 2024, we lost all but three of our commercial cleaning accounts, our employees vanished without warning, and we faced enormous losses in real estate. One contractor stole thousands of dollars from us in a deal gone bad. Our credit cards were maxed out, and our financial situation spiraled out of control.

We lost our health insurance and faced mounting shut-off notices, vehicle repossession threats, overdrawn bank accounts, and foreclosure on our home. Some days, we had less than $15 in our bank account, living off gift cards just to feed our family of four. It felt like everything was falling apart.

But here's the thing about prophetic preparation: it requires you to keep going, even when everything around you tell you to stop. You must prepare for the promise of God, even when your current situation looks like anything but a promise.

My wife and I had days where we wanted to throw in the towel. We were emotionally drained, physically exhausted, and spiritually broken. But after the tears fell, after the moments of doubt, we knew we had to stay obedient to God's will. Faith is not truly faith until it looks ridiculous to the natural eye. The weapons were formed, no doubt, but God promised they wouldn't prosper.

In the midst of our lowest moments, God would send us reminders and confirmations to stay the course. Sometimes it came through a word from a friend, sometimes in a message we heard, and sometimes it was simply a feeling deep in our hearts that said, "Don't give up." Those reminders kept us aligned with the vision, even when everything in our lives seemed contrary to that promise. That season broke us, yes, but it also revealed how much we weren't trusting God. We had to learn that the delays we were experiencing were not denials—they were for our development.

And here's the key: that season wasn't just about us. It was preparation for the people we were meant to inspire—you. Every tear we shed, every obstacle we faced, every painful lesson we learned, it was all to tell you this today: **DO NOT GIVE UP**. The struggle isn't just your story; it's part of the prophetic preparation for your destiny. The way you prepare today speaks directly to the future God has for you. Your preparation is a declaration that you believe in the vision He's given you.

Look at the Bible. Every great move of God was preceded by preparation. Noah didn't build the ark after the rain started—he spent years building it while the skies were clear. Joseph didn't just rise to power in Egypt overnight—he spent years in slavery and prison, learning humility and leadership, before he was ready to save a nation. Even Jesus spent 30 years in preparation for a three-year ministry that would change the course of history. So, why do we think we can skip the process?

The process—the refinement—is not meant to destroy you. It's meant to burn off what's keeping you bound. God's refinery doesn't come to burn you down, but to build you up. He strips away the layers of fear, doubt, pride, and control so that you can step into your purpose fully free and fully equipped.

If there is one thing you take away from this chapter, let it be this: **Storms are only temporary**, as it says in 2 Corinthians 4:17, "our light afflictions are but for a moment." **Storms are teachers**, as Psalm 119:71 reminds us, "It was good for me to be afflicted so that I might learn your decrees." **And storms are transportation devices carrying us to the next level** as James 1:2-3 teaches, "Consider it pure joy, my brothers and sisters, whenever you face trials of many kinds, because you know that the testing of your faith produces perseverance."

This is the essence of prophetic preparation—it's not just about enduring the storm but understanding that the storm itself is a vehicle for your growth. What you're going through today is shaping you for the vision God has for tomorrow. Every setback is part of the setup for your breakthrough. Every loss is a lesson. Every delay is divine timing.

The key to prophetic preparation is simple: **#KEEPGOING**. Even when it doesn't make sense. Even when you feel like you're at the end of your strength. Even when the doors keep closing and the world tells you to quit. Keep going. God's promises are on the other side of your obedience. The preparation may be painful, but the harvest will be plentiful.

So, I ask you: What are you preparing for? What vision has God planted in your heart that feels too big, too distant, too impossible? Keep going. Build while you're waiting. Prepare while you're in the storm. And trust that when the time is right, the seed you've been sowing will take root, and it will grow into something greater than you could have ever imagined.

If Storms are teachers, what are some storms you have experienced and how did you get through them?

_____
_____
_____
_____
_____
_____
_____
_____
_____
_____
_____
_____
_____
_____
_____
_____
_____
_____
_____
_____
_____
_____
_____
_____
_____
_____
_____
_____
_____
_____
_____
_____
_____
_____
_____

CHAPTER 8: #KEEPGOING

The image below illustrates transparency. There's a massive pile of bills on my desk that was disheartening to open……per Ecclesiastes 3:1-8, please know there is a season for everything, and you are not alone!

You may hear us say, see us wear, or intentionally proclaim the #keepgoing mantra. To us, this is not just some trendy saying tied to The Just-In Time Brand, this mantra is our lifestyle; a heavy burden that we carry. In the journey of entrepreneurship, there will be moments when everything feels like it's falling apart.

I'm not talking about the usual stress or challenges that come with running a business—I'm talking about the kind of storms that make you question your very path. For us, that season came in waves that seemed relentless, and the hits kept coming from every direction, with no break.

We lost all but three of our commercial cleaning clients at Just-In Time Cleaning, and our income took a massive hit with Just-In Time Investments. But that was only the beginning. My wife Tia, the cornerstone of our family and business, suddenly needed emergency heart surgery in 2023.

I remember the fear in her eyes, and the helplessness I felt as doctors told us that fluid had surrounded her heart, making it difficult for her to breathe and this required immediate action for her to survive. At that moment, nothing else mattered except her survival, but as the storm of life would have it, our healthcare coverage had lapsed, leaving us exposed. That day, as I sat by her side in the hospital, I questioned everything. Was I doing enough to protect her? To protect our family?

As if that weren't enough, before Tia needed emergency surgery, we hired a contractor for one of our real estate flips who turned out to be nothing short of a nightmare. The contractors' negligence and dishonesty cost us thousands of dollars, pushing us deeper into financial distress. All our credit cards were maxed out, every single one.

The businesses that we had built with blood, sweat, and tears were hanging by a thread. There were days when we couldn't even afford the basics, living off gift cards just to get through the week. Meanwhile, the bills kept piling up on our desk, each one a reminder of how much we were sinking. Bill collectors were merciless, calling day and night, adding insult to injury.

Then, one of the most terrifying moments of my life happened. Tia and our children were hit by a driver who had fallen asleep at the wheel. In that moment, I felt as though the weight of the world was crushing me. I couldn't lose them. I couldn't take another hit. Yet, during one of the most embarrassing and gut-wrenching seasons of our lives, our home was scheduled for foreclosure.

I remember looking at Tia, and whispering the question in my heart, *"how did we get here"*? In 2016, we had started with so much hope, so much faith, and now I felt like we were drowning in failure.

There were days when it felt as though our best days were behind us. We had fallen into a deep pit of uncertainty, and I wasn't sure if we had the strength or the faith to climb out. I remember sitting at my desk, staring at the pile of bills, and wondering if we were still on the right path.

Had we misunderstood God's calling? Were we failing because we had strayed from His plan? Transparently speaking, "faith fatigue" tried to settle in. It's that moment when you've fought so long and so hard that your faith feels worn out, like an old threadbare rope about to snap.

But deep down, in the midst of the doubt trying to creep in, we knew God had told us to start these businesses. He didn't promise it would be easy, but He did promise that He would be with us. And if there's one thing we've learned in this journey, it's that God doesn't bring you this far just to leave you.

We had to keep going, even when it felt impossible. We had to build in the face of opposition, just like Noah did when God told him to build an ark, though no one had ever seen rain like that before. Can you imagine the ridicule he faced? Yet, he kept building. Why? Because God had spoken.

It reminded me of Moses, standing at the edge of the Red Sea, with Pharaoh's army closing in behind him. He had led the Israelites out of Egypt, following God's command, but now he was staring at an impossibility—a sea too vast to cross. Yet, in that moment of fear and doubt, God parted the waters.

The Red Sea wasn't the end; it was the beginning of deliverance. The question is, can you #keepgoing while staring at your Red Sea?

Can you move forward when everything in front of you seems impassable?

Faith in entrepreneurship is no different. It's about trusting the vision God gave you, even when the path forward looks like a dead end.

It's about holding onto the promise, even when your resources have run dry, when the clients are few, and when your health or the health of your loved ones is threatened. In those moments, it's not about what you can see, but about what you know. We knew God was faithful. We knew He hadn't abandoned us, even when it felt like we were walking through a valley of defeat.

Tia and I had to make a choice. Were we going to let the storm drown us, or were we going to keep building in the rain? We chose to keep building in the rain! The opposition was fierce, but every time we thought about giving up, God would send a word, a reminder, or an unexpected blessing to let us know we weren't alone.

He would even give us a word to give to someone else! How about that?! He was with us, just as He was with Joseph when he was betrayed by his brothers and thrown into a pit. Joseph didn't give up. Even in the pit, in prison, and in every setback, he prepared for the moment when God would elevate him to be the second most powerful man in Egypt.

We had to cling to the promise that our setbacks were setting us up for something greater. Just like those who came before us, we had to be willing to weather the storm, to build even when everything around us looked like it was falling apart. That's the heart of prophetic preparation—it's believing that what God said is coming, even when all the signs say otherwise.

If you're in a season where it feels like everything is against you, let me encourage you: **KeepGoing**. Though recalling and sharing this difficult season brings tears to my eyes, I know that through transparency, you can be freed from the enemy's lies.

God wouldn't tell you to build if He didn't have something waiting for you on the other side. The Red Sea wasn't the Israelites' end, it was the gateway to their promised land. Don't let the storm make you forget the promise. Keep building, keep trusting, keep believing. God is with you in the storm, just as He was with us. He honored us— that season of our lives was our proving ground.

Just as God tested Abraham, He tested us, asking if we were willing to lay our "Isaacs" on the altar. It was only then that He provided a ram in the bush. Can God trust you with the weight, while you wait? I want you to remember this: anything God calls you to do will come with cups of suffering, thorns of hardship, and a necessary sifting to refine your mantle into something authentic, humble, and powerful.

This chapter of our lives wasn't just for us, **it's for you**. It's a reminder that no matter how difficult things become, God is faithful to complete the work He began in you, as He promises in Philippians 1:6 and Jeremiah 29:11. So, when you find yourself standing at your own Red Sea, staring at what seems impossible, remember: God didn't bring you this far to leave you. He's preparing you for something greater. #keepgoing

Have you ever felt like you misunderstood God's calling on your life? How did you figure out that his call was?

_____
_____
_____
_____
_____
_____
_____
_____
_____
_____
_____
_____
_____
_____
_____
_____
_____
_____
_____
_____
_____
_____
_____
_____
_____
_____
_____
_____
_____
_____
_____
_____

The Price of Success: What are you Willing to Pay?

CHAPTER 9: See It Before You See It

"You must see it before you see it." These are the words of Karen Clark Sheard, and they hold more truth than we realize at first glance. How can you see something that isn't there? How can you believe in something when all evidence points to its absence? Yet, this is the crux of faith, the ability to see with spiritual eyes what is not yet visible in the physical world.

It's the ability to believe in your vision so deeply that you act on it, build it, and nurture it as if it's already fully realized. Faith requires you to see what others can't, and even what you can't physically see yet, and believe that it's coming to pass.

I want to share something that's key to building a future you can't see yet: the bigger your vision, the greater the preparation and cleanup will be. Imagine a construction site. The foundation is being laid, and there's debris everywhere. It's messy, incomplete, and chaotic. But the builders know what they're creating. They don't wait for the project to be finished before they start working as if it's already complete.

They see the finished product in their minds and work accordingly. Your vision works the same way—you must start working now, operating as if the vision is already fully functional. Even if you feel like nothing is happening yet, you're laying the groundwork for something much bigger.

Hebrews 11:1 tells us, "Now faith is the substance of things hoped for, the evidence of things not seen." If you don't believe in your own vision, how can you expect others to? You must believe it for yourself first. Let that sink in: you must believe it before you see it. Your dreams cannot stay locked inside your mind. They need to be spoken, acted upon, and nurtured.

There's an old saying I used to hear as a young man, one that I never fully grasped until now: "If you build it, they will come." It's tempting to wait until everything feels perfect—until all the pieces are in place, until the finances are secure, until you feel more ready. But that day may never come. If you keep putting it off, you'll always find a new excuse to wait. Instead of giving yourself reasons why it can't happen, start giving yourself reasons why it will.

The Bible reminds us in Habakkuk 2:2, "Write the vision, and make it plain upon tables, that he may run that readeth it."

Write your goals down. Put them where you can see them every day. Don't just glance at them—speak them out loud. Declare them over your life. Faith to start is all you need. Faith to keep going is the key to unlocking what God has in store for you.

Turn your opposition into opportunity, your doubt into belief, your fear into courage. The power to change your reality is in your hands. Often, when a new building is under construction, you'll see a rendering of the finished product posted outside the messy construction zone. That image is there to show you what's coming, even though all you can see at the moment is dirt and chaos.

Your words, your faith, and your actions are like that rendering. They declare what's coming before it arrives. You don't need a sign on your forehead or an announcement to the world. Let the words you speak be the sign of what's happening in your heart and mind.

But here's the catch: there's an expiration date on opportunity. If you let too much time pass without acting, you might miss your moment. Just like with food, if you wait too long past the expiration date, it spoils. That's when you end up throwing away what could've been, only to go back and buy something you could've had all along. Are you willing to pay the price again, or are you ready to get up and accomplish what you've been called to do right now?

It may seem crazy now but trust me—it's worth it. Richard Branson once said, *"If your dreams don't scare you, they're too small."* Sometimes, the craziest ideas, the most outlandish dreams, are the very ones God has planted in you for a purpose. It's not always about what others see. It's about what you see.

Think of the two rabbits in a familiar picture—one has a large carrot top above the ground, but it's all leaves. The other has a small carrot top, but beneath the soil, there's a massive carrot growing. From the outside, it looks like the first rabbit is winning, but the second one holds the true treasure. Success isn't always about what's visible to others. It's about the work being done in the unseen. You're cultivating something deep, something meaningful, and when it's time, the world will see the full fruit of your labor.

Quitting should never be an option. Sure, the thought might cross your mind—after all, we're human. But you can control how much you let those thoughts settle in. Psalms 19:4 says, "Let the words of my mouth and the meditation of my heart be acceptable in thy sight." What are you meditating on? Just because you don't speak your fears out loud doesn't mean they aren't affecting you. You have to replace those silent doubts with faith-filled declarations.

Think of Noah. He preached about rain for years, and nothing happened while he built the ark. But Noah kept building because he believed in the rain, even when no one else did. The rain didn't come until he was finished, and because he prepared for it, he and his family were spared from the flood. Are you preparing for your present and future? Are you building your "ark" while others doubt?

Plant the seeds of belief now, while the soil is fertile. Don't waste time planting in dead ground. Take your time, be patient, and most of all, stay in prayer. Pray, think, and pray again. Keep going back to God with your dreams until you're a believer in your own destiny. The harvest will come, but only if you're willing to put in the work today, seeing the end result before it even begins to sprout.

In the end, success isn't just about what others see—it's about what you believe. Speak it, see it, and watch as God brings it to pass. You've already been equipped for the journey ahead. Now, it's time to build.

What does this scripture mean to you, "Now faith is the substance of things hoped for, the evidence of things not seen."

_____
_____
_____
_____
_____
_____
_____
_____
_____
_____
_____
_____
_____
_____
_____
_____
_____
_____
_____
_____
_____
_____
_____
_____
_____
_____
_____
_____
_____
_____
_____
_____
_____
_____

What are you building while others are doubting you?

_____

_____

_____

_____

_____

_____

_____

_____

_____

_____

_____

_____

_____

_____

_____

_____

_____

_____

_____

_____

_____

_____

_____

_____

_____

_____

_____

_____

_____

_____

_____

_____

_____

_____

_____

_____

_____

CHAPTER 10: God Wants Your Trust!

Trust is not easy. It's one of those words that sounds simple but feels impossible in practice. We've all heard someone say, "Just trust God." But what happens when your trust has been shattered by life's blows? What happens when you feel like you've done all you can, but you're still standing in the middle of a storm with no shelter in sight?

For us, trust wasn't something that came naturally. It was something we had to learn, and honestly, it's still something we wrestle with. Our journey with *Just-In Time* wasn't just about learning how to run a business — it was about learning how to trust God when everything around us was screaming that we should quit. And let me tell you, it wasn't easy.

There were seasons when we felt like we were stuck in a whirlwind of defeat. It wasn't one thing — it was everything. We watched our business accounts drain to nearly nothing. We were down to using Dollar Tree gift cards to buy groceries. Let that sink in for a moment. We were building multiple businesses but couldn't afford to buy proper groceries. If that wasn't bad enough, our business partners betrayed us. People we trusted — people we shared visions with — turned on us. They left us with unpaid invoices, failed promises, and emotional wounds that shook our confidence. We had employees who ghosted us with no warning, leaving us to fulfill contracts alone.

And then came the day that still haunts me. We had been dodging calls from creditors for weeks. Every time the phone rang, it felt like a punch to the gut. That day, I looked outside and saw the repossession company pulling into our driveway. My heart sank. My wife, Tia, had just been in a car accident with our children only a few hours earlier, and now a tow truck was coming to take our family vehicle. I stood there, numb, in disbelief, asking God "Why us"? Why now? Thankfully, the vehicle was in a tow yard waiting on the insurance to pick it up for repairs.

I'm going to be honest with you, at that moment, I questioned everything. I questioned if I'd heard God correctly when He told us to start these businesses. I questioned if I was fit to be a husband, a father, and a leader. I questioned if I had failed my family.

The pain was so deep, but it taught me something I'll never forget. **God wants your trust, especially when it looks like everything is falling apart.** Trust is not about the absence of storms. It's about believing God is still in control while the storm is raging. It's about clinging to His promises even when life looks like chaos.

The same God that shut the mouths of lions for Daniel, the same God who parted the Red Sea for Moses — that same God is working behind the scenes of your life.

I need you to ask yourself a question right now: **Can you trust God while staring at a Red Sea?** Picture it. You're standing at the edge of the sea, and behind you is Pharaoh's army charging toward you. You see no bridge, no exit, and no place to run. Would you trust God then? The truth is, most of us wouldn't.

Most of us would panic, just like the Israelites did. But this is where trust is born. It's in the moment when there's no way out that God makes a way. It's in the moment when everything feels like it's closing in that He parts the sea in front of you. But here's the part we often miss — the sea didn't part *until Moses stretched out his hand*. The power was in the stretch. The stretch was an act of trust. Are you willing to stretch when it doesn't make sense?

God is not asking you to have it all figured out. He's just asking for your trust. He's not asking you to know every step. He's asking you to take the first one. You see, faith without works is dead, and trust without action is just words. We had to put our trust into action. We had to keep building Just-In Time even when our accounts were in the negative. We had to keep paying employees even when we didn't know how we would pay ourselves. We had to keep answering those creditor calls with honesty and dignity, trusting that God would provide.

Sometimes we think that if God tells us to build something, then it should be easy. Wrong! If you look through scripture, you'll see that every major assignment from God came with opposition. Noah had to build an ark when there wasn't a single cloud in the sky. Abraham had to climb a mountain with his son Isaac, fully expecting to sacrifice him. Joseph was thrown into a pit by his brothers and later sat in prison for years. But here's the key: The opposition was a test, not a punishment. The ark still floated. The ram still appeared. Joseph still rose to second-in-command. God never leaves you in the test. He walks you through it.

If you're reading this and you feel like you're drowning, I want to encourage you. This is not permanent. It's a test. You're not going to stay in this valley. You may feel like you've been knocked down, but the Word of God says, *"The righteous may fall seven times, but they rise again."* (Proverbs 24:16) If you can rise one more time, God can turn it around.

I'm reminded of a story from my childhood. My mother had 10 children, and after my father passed away, she raised us on her own.

We didn't have much, but we had faith. I remember my stepfather Ray, stepping into our lives and teaching us lessons about patience, trust, and hard work. He wasn't a man of many words, but his actions spoke louder than sermons. He trusted God, and he taught us to do the same. I still hear his voice in my head when I'm on the brink of quitting. "Don't give up."

God wants your trust. He's not looking for perfection. He's looking for progress. He's not asking you to know every step of the journey — He just wants you to take the next one. Remember, the Israelites didn't have GPS when they were walking to the Promised Land. They had to trust God every day for direction. And just like them, you may not have a clear roadmap for your success. But guess what? God does.

Here's the reality: You will have to endure some losses. But losses are not punishments. Losses are lessons. The bad business partners that betrayed us taught us how to vet people better. The attempted car repossession taught us to never let debt control us. The loss of clients taught us how to diversify our income streams. Every loss had a lesson attached to it. The pain was real, but so was the progress.

Don't be afraid to lose. Be afraid to stay the same.

I want to leave you with this image. Imagine you're a construction worker building a skyscraper. Day by day, you're laying down bricks. It feels slow, and some days you wonder if you're making any progress. But here's what you can't see — every single brick matters. Every step of trust you take matters. Every prayer you pray matters. Every late night spent planning matters. The building is rising, even if you can't see it.

The key to this whole chapter is this: **God wants your trust.** He wants your faith in Him to be so unshakable that even when life takes a blow, you stand firm. Just like Paul, you might have a thorn in your side that you've begged God to remove. But remember what God told Paul: "My grace is sufficient for you, for my power is made perfect in weakness." (2 Corinthians 12:9)

Your weakness is not the end of your story. Your failure is not the end of your business. Your brokenness is not your identity. God is in the restoration business.

Now that you've made it this far, I want you to pause for a moment. Take a deep breath. Look at everything you've been through. You're still here. You've made it through every storm, every setback, and every betrayal. And guess what? You're stronger than you think.

But now it's time for something new. Get ready, because what's ahead is better than what's behind. God didn't bring you through the fire just for you to smell like smoke. He brought you through to show you that you're fireproof. #keepgoing!

Has God ever told you something and you questioned if it was your voice or His? Write about it here.

_____
_____
_____
_____
_____
_____
_____
_____
_____
_____
_____
_____
_____
_____
_____
_____
_____
_____
_____
_____
_____
_____
_____
_____
_____
_____
_____
_____
_____
_____

The Price of Success: What are you Willing to Pay?

CHAPTER 11:

Delayed Not Denied

Delays can feel like punishment. They can make you question everything you've ever believed about yourself, your abilities, and even your faith. It's hard to trust God when everything you've worked for seems to be slipping out of your hands. But here's what I need you to understand: a delay is not a denial. It's simply a pause, a divine redirection, or, better yet, a process of preparation.

When God has a calling on your life, He's not just interested in where you're going — He's equally invested in *who you're becoming* along the way. It's easy to want success, but success without character can become a curse. This is why God doesn't want your gift to take you where your character can't keep you. **Success requires structure. Success requires maturity. Success requires patience**. And all three of these are built during seasons of delay.

The enemy wants you to believe that delays mean denial. But that's a lie. Just because something didn't happen when you wanted it to doesn't mean it won't happen at all. If you're standing in the middle of a delay right now, I want you to hear me clearly: Your promise is still coming. Just like Joseph was delayed in the prison before becoming second-in-command of Egypt, and just like David was delayed in the fields before being crowned king, your delay is part of God's divine process. You're being developed for destiny.

There's a story I love about squatters. Squatters are people who occupy property that doesn't belong to them. And if the owner of that property doesn't remove them within a certain amount of time, the squatter gains "squatters' rights" — legally allowing them to stay there. Can I ask you something? How many squatters have you allowed to stay in your mind rent-free? I'm talking about fear, doubt, insecurity, and feelings of inadequacy.

Every day you let these squatters stay in your mind, they claim more rights over your thoughts. It's time to evict them. The only reason negativity is still squatting in your mind is because you haven't demanded it leave. But here's the good news: You have the authority to kick them out.

The Word of God says in 2 Corinthians 10:5, "We demolish arguments and every pretension that sets itself up against the knowledge of God, and we take captive every thought to make it obedient to Christ." In other words, you are the landlord of your mind. If negative thoughts are occupying space, you have the power to evict them. Don't let negativity squat in a space that's reserved for faith, confidence, and strategy. A mind full of doubt cannot produce a life full of success.

Character over Gifts

One of the most profound lessons I've learned is this: God's delays are about building your character, not breaking your spirit. So many people want the platform, but they don't want the process. They want the promise, but they don't want the preparation. It's no coincidence that every person in the Bible who was called to greatness had to wait. God won't let you skip steps because shortcuts rob you of strength. Joseph wasn't just delayed in prison — he was being prepared for leadership. David wasn't just delayed as a shepherd boy — he was being trained to be a king. And just like them, you're not just waiting — **you're being established.**

Being "established" is different from just "being successful." When something is established, it is unshakable, immovable, and grounded. Being established means you're not only successful in your craft but also in your character. And I'll be honest with you, character-building hurts. It's uncomfortable, it's lonely, and sometimes it feels unfair. But I'd rather be established than be successful for a season. Success without character is a scandal waiting to happen. Character will sustain you when success tries to break you.

God will not promote you prematurely. Think about that for a second. What if He gave you everything you prayed for right now, but you weren't ready for it? Would it crush you? Would you lose it all because you didn't have the wisdom, patience, or humility to maintain it? God is not punishing you with this delay. He's protecting you. He's building something in you that will allow you to sustain what's coming. Every ounce of pain you've experienced is shaping your story, your voice, and your heart. It's not just about what you build — it's about who you become while building it.

Impact Over Income

Let's be clear. Success is not just about making more money. Success is about making an impact. When you're established, you no longer chase checks — you chase change. You shift from focusing on *what you can get* to *what you can give*. That shift in thinking is the evidence of true establishment. **God is calling you to be a blessing to others.**

Look at what God told Abraham in Genesis 12:2: "I will bless you... and you will be a blessing." When God calls you to success, it's not just for you. It's so that you can be a blessing to your community, your family, and the world. If your vision only includes you, it's too small. True success is about impact, legacy, and transformation.

74

During our most stressful, daunting seasons, something shifted when we stopped focusing on survival and started focusing on service. When we shifted from "How can we get out of this?" to "How can we serve others during this?" God began to move in our lives. Our perspective shifted, and so did our strategy. Service opens the door to success.

5 Keys To Remember When You Feel Delayed

1. **Character Must Be Developed** – Your gifts will get you in the door, but your character will keep you in the room.
2. **Evict The Squatters** – Don't allow fear, doubt, or anxiety to squat in your mind. Take control.
3. **Trust The Timing** – God knows when you're ready. If it's delayed, it's because He's preparing something better.
4. **Impact Over Income** – Your calling is about impact, not just a paycheck. Be a vessel for others.
5. **The Blessing Is In The Wait** – Delays aren't denials. They're divine appointments to build you, not break you.

Trust The Process, Embrace the Journey
If you take anything away from this chapter, let it be this: God's delay is not His denial. You are being established. The wait is not wasted. Just like a house built on a solid foundation can withstand the storm, you are being built to last. God is preparing you so that when the blessing comes, it won't crush you. He's not just giving you success — He's making you unshakable. So, when the tests come, stand firm.

I leave you with this final thought: You are closer than you think. Right now, you are on the edge of something great. Don't you dare give up. Delayed does not mean denied. It means you're being developed. It means you're being established. It means you're being strengthened for what's to come. And what's to come is far greater than what you're leaving behind.

"Success is about making an impact." What impact are you looking to make?

_____

_____

_____

_____

_____

_____

_____

_____

_____

_____

_____

_____

_____

_____

_____

_____

_____

_____

_____

_____

_____

_____

_____

_____

_____

_____

_____

_____

_____

_____

_____

_____

CHAPTER 12: Replenish

"And I will restore to you the years that the locust hath eaten, the cankerworm, and the caterpillar, and the palmerworm, my great army which I sent among you."
– Joel 2:25 (KJV)

What does it truly mean to replenish? According to Webster's dictionary, it means "to fill or build up again." But I want you to think deeper than that definition. It's not just about refilling what's empty—it's about being restored to a state that's stronger than before. Imagine a glass that's been shattered into pieces. Restoration doesn't just mean gluing the pieces back together, it means being made whole, even better than before.

After seasons of severe trials, it's natural to feel depleted—spiritually, mentally, emotionally, and even financially. If you've ever walked through a wilderness season where everything that could go wrong *did* go wrong, then you know exactly what I'm talking about.

When you've lost health, resources, clients, contracts, finances, energy, momentum, and confidence, you begin to wonder how you'll ever recover. But here's the truth: God never allows loss without preparing a season of restoration.

The Mind Must Be Replenished First

Nothing in your life can be replenished physically until it is first replenished mentally. Everything you see in your life, your business, your relationships, your health—started as a thought. Scripture reminds us in Proverbs 23:7, "For as he thinketh in his heart, so is he." If your mind is stuck on lack, fear, and defeat, then that's exactly what will manifest in your life. But if your mind is refreshed, restored, and focused on abundance, faith, and victory, everything around you will follow suit.

Have you ever refreshed a page on the internet? When content is outdated or the page is lagging, there's an option in the upper corner to press "refresh." And what happens when you press it? The old, outdated information is clear, and fresh, relevant content appears. Your mind operates the same way. If you continue to replay past mistakes, failures, and disappointments, you will stay stuck in a loop of outdated information. But if you press the "refresh" button in your mind, you give yourself permission to see things differently.

This is where God steps in. He wants to renew your mind. Romans 12:2 says, "Do not conform to the pattern of this world, but be transformed by the renewing of your mind." Your mind needs renewal just as much as your spirit. Why? Because your mind is the battlefield where doubt, fear, and negativity try to take root. But you have the power to press refresh. God is ready to fill you with new thoughts, new strategies, and new ideas. But you must be willing to let go of the outdated content in your mind and receive what He is offering.

Replenishing Your Heart and Spirit

After severe trials, your heart often feels drained. It's not just your energy that's depleted, it's your hope. Discouragement can sneak in after too many "no's," too many setbacks, and too many delays. But I need you to hear this: God is not done with you. In fact, every setback you've faced has been a setup for a greater comeback.

When I think of replenishment, I think of Elijah. After calling down fire from heaven and defeating the prophets of Baal, he found himself emotionally exhausted, hiding in a cave, and wanting to give up. He told God, "I have had enough, Lord. Take my life." (1 Kings 19:4) But instead of granting his request, God did something better— He sent an angel to feed him. The angel didn't give Elijah a lecture; he gave him *rest* and *nourishment*. After being restored, Elijah had the strength to continue his journey.

God wants to do the same for you. You may feel like you've done all you can do. You've fought, built, sacrificed, and endured, but it feels like nothing is working. You've been strong for so long that now you feel too weak to keep going. But hear me when I say this: God sees you, and He is sending you a divine refill. Just as the angel came to Elijah, help is on the way. This is your season to be replenished spiritually, mentally, and emotionally.

Replenishing Your Marketplace. The enemy would love for you to believe that the losses you've experienced in your business are permanent. He'll try to convince you that you're too far gone to recover. But remember this: Loss is temporary, but God's restoration is eternal.

You may have lost clients, accounts, contracts, or even revenue, but what's coming is better than what was lost. Joel 2:25 says, "I will restore to you the years that the locust has eaten." Think about that. The locust didn't just eat fruit—it ate years. It devoured time. But God promises that He will restore not only the harvest but also the *years* that were lost. If you've ever felt like you lost time, opportunities, or momentum, this scripture is for you. God doesn't just give back things; He gives back *time*.

Here's something God revealed to me: Sometimes, He will let everything fall apart just to show you that you were never in control. When you're stripped of your own strength, you realize that it was never your strength sustaining you in the first place. It was God. And when He restores you, He doesn't just give you back what you had—He gives you double for your trouble. Look at Job. He lost his family, his wealth, and his health, but when God restored him, He gave him twice as much as he had before. (Job 42:10)

God will do the same for you. Your business may have lost revenue, but don't be surprised when new contracts, new clients, and new opportunities come pouring in. This is the season of replenishment.

Replenishing Your Belief

One of the biggest things that needs to be replenished after a season of trials is your belief in yourself. Trials have a way of chipping away at your confidence. You start to second-guess your decisions and doubt your abilities. But let me tell you something: God did not bring you this far to leave you.

If you've ever felt like you're empty, like you have nothing left to give, it's time to remember that God has already placed everything you need inside of you. The reason you need to be replenished is because you were already full. You can't refill something that was never filled in the first place. The fact that you're feeling empty means you were once overflowing. **God doesn't replenish empty vessels—He refills vessels that were once full.**

So, don't be discouraged when you feel drained. It's a sign that you've been pouring out into others. Just as water is essential to the human body, your gifts, talents, and creativity are essential to the people assigned to you. **You are the water someone needs.** Your vision, your ideas, and your perseverance are the life source that someone else is waiting for. Don't let fear or fatigue cause you to withhold the water. Pray, press refresh, and trust that God is filling you back up.

The Replenishment Promise

As you close this chapter, I want you to remember this: Replenishment is God's promise to you. If you feel like everything is running dry—your finances, your faith, your energy—know that God is about to send a refill. The only thing you need to do is stay in position. Don't give up before the rain comes. Noah didn't stop building the ark because he hadn't seen rain yet. He trusted that rain was on the way, and because of that faith, he was ready when the flood came.

If you're reading this and you feel like you're in a dry season, remember that dry seasons don't last forever. There's an outpour coming. Your faith is the cup that will catch the rain. Don't put your cup away just because it hasn't started raining yet. The rain is coming.

God is going to replenish you mentally, spiritually, emotionally, and financially. The ideas that once seemed out of reach are within your grasp. The contracts you lost will be replaced with larger ones. The faith you thought had run dry will be renewed. You are not forgotten, and you are not finished. God is going to restore every single thing you thought you lost.

This is your season of replenishment. Get ready. **The rain is coming.**

"For as he thinketh in his heart, so is he." What is it that you think of yourself?

_____
_____
_____
_____
_____
_____
_____
_____
_____
_____
_____
_____
_____
_____
_____
_____
_____
_____
_____
_____
_____
_____
_____
_____
_____
_____
_____
_____
_____
_____
_____
_____

"The only thing you need to do is stay in position." How will you stay in position and wait for your blessing?

_____

_____

_____

_____

_____

_____

_____

_____

_____

_____

_____

_____

_____

_____

_____

_____

_____

_____

_____

_____

_____

_____

_____

_____

_____

_____

_____

_____

_____

_____

_____

CLOSING PRAYER

Heavenly Father, in the name of Jesus Christ, I come before You with a heart full of gratitude. I pray for every reader who has journeyed through the pages of this book. Lord, I ask that You bless them abundantly with prosperity, wisdom, and clarity. For every ounce of doubt they have faced, I ask that You transform it into unwavering belief. Turn their fear into courage, Lord. Remind them that You are omnipresent—You are with them in their minds, their hearts, and their thoughts. Let them become vessels for Your glory, shining examples of Your power and purpose.

Father, I know the road may get rough at times, and there will be moments when it feels like quitting is the only option. But You declared in Your Word that *"He who began a good work in you will carry it on to completion until the day of Christ Jesus."* (Philippians 1:6) So, I ask that You strengthen their faith and remind them that You finish what You start. Surround them with Your shekinah glory, Lord. Cover them with Your peace, protection, and power.

God, I know You to be a healer, a deliverer, a mind regulator, a doctor, a lawyer, a nurse, and whatever else Your people need You to be. Do for them what You have done for me, Lord. Let their lives be a living testimony of Your faithfulness. I pray that these words are not just read but felt deeply in their hearts. Stir something within them that cannot be shaken.

I thank You in advance, Father, for the testimonies that will follow this book. I thank You for stories of success, for breakthroughs, for perseverance, and for renewed strength. But most of all, Lord, I thank You for every reader who will either find, restore, or strengthen their relationship with You. Let them know that every step of their journey is part of Your divine plan, and they are never alone.

In the name of Jesus Christ, we pray. Amen.

There is a price for success—are you willing to pay it for God's glory?

KEEP GOING! Go in peace, and know that even though we may never meet, I am praying that the blessings of the Lord will cover your home and your family. From my family to yours, **God bless you!**

∾

About the Authors

Justin and Tia Mason are entrepreneurs, visionaries, and faith-driven leaders who have built their success on resilience, perseverance, and unwavering trust in God. Married and deeply rooted in their shared purpose, they founded Just-In Time in 2016—starting with a single cleaning service and expanding into a multifaceted business empire.

Through every challenge, hardship, and moment of uncertainty, they discovered the true Price of Success—a journey of faith, sacrifice, and relentless determination. Their mission is to inspire and equip entrepreneurs, trailblazers, and dreamers to push beyond their limits of comfortability.

Logos over time

www.ingramcontent com/pod-product-compliance
Lightning Source LLC
Chambersburg PA
CBRC090837120626
46551CB00007B/681